Millennium Kopprasch Series

PREPARATORY KOPPRASCH

Horn Etudes

Jeffrey Agrell

Copyright © 2018 by Jeffrey Agrell

All rights reserved. No part of this book, including interior design, cover design, logos, and icons may be reproduced or transmitted in any form, by any means (electronic, photocopying, recording, or otherwise) without the prior consent of the publisher except for brief quotations in a book review. "Wildwind Editions" and the Wildwind Editions logo are trademarks of Wildwind Editions.

Published by Wildwind Editions
Layout and formatting by Awadhesh Yadav

First Printing: 2018

ISBN-13: 978-1722165512
ISBN-10: 1722165510

Books by Jeffrey Agrell

Harmony Kopprasch

Rhythm Kopprasch

Horn Technique

The Creative Hornist

Improvisation Games for Classical Musicians (2008)

Improvisation Games for Classical Musicians, Vol. II (2016)

Improvised Chamber Music for Classical Musicians

Improv Games for One Player

Improv Duets for Classical Musicians

Vocal Improvisation Games
(with co-author Patrice Madura)

Creative Pedagogy for Piano Teachers
(with co-author Aura Strohschein)

The Millennium Kopprasch Series

I know what you're thinking: What? Messing with Kopprasch? Why? Is that even legal? Please explain!

I'm glad you asked those questions. What we familiarly and simply call "Kopprasch" refers to the etude collection of 60 studies for low horn Op. 6 by German composer Georg Kopprasch (ca. 1800 - c. 1850). Kopprasch was a professional hornist whose career included playing in the Royal Berlin Theater Orchestra (after 1822) and the court orchestra of the Prince of Dessau (after 1832). His sixty etudes (published in two volumes) were some of the earliest etudes published for the newly invented valve horn, and are still arguably the most popular etudes for horn (as well as being regularly poached by other brasses) today.

The etudes are often quite "mechanical" in nature (with a couple of exceptions), and are essentially various elaborations of the most basic musical material: scales and arpeggios. All well and good, and still useful today, but there is one inescapable problem: a few things have changed in both the real and the musical world since the early 19th century. It goes without saying (so we will say it): the musician of the new millennium can expect to face technical and musical challenges that far exceed the basics covered by Kopprasch.

What we do in The Millennium Kopprasch Series is to take the familiar and stretch it, that is, we take Kopprasch's etudes and dramatically extend them in various ways (through this series) so that the millennium musician acquires the depth and breadth they need to survive and thrive almost two hundred years after those first original etudes were written. Look around: how many things do you see are the same as they were in 1830? Transportation. Food. Science. Communication. Clothing. Musical styles. Medicine. Sports. Anything electric. And on and on. It requires no great effort to see the tremendous differences. Hence this series, which simply asks: *shouldn't musical studies reflect the demands of the current era?*

The Millennium Kopprasch Series will (theoretically) eventually comprise about ten two-volume sets of Kopprasch (heretofore our shorthand term for the etude collection), in two volumes for each version to mirror the originals. *Rhythm Kopprasch* was the first of these re-imagined etudes, followed by *Harmony Kopprasch*. Both of these are more challenging than the originals; *Preparatory Kopprasch* is deliberately much easier than the original etudes, since the goal here is to provide stepping stones for young players by introducing them to simplified versions of the originals.

Subsequent volumes in the MK Series will appear every few months for the next several years. Stay tuned, and be the first on your block to collect the entire series!

PS: send us your email address if you would like to be informed when the next set is published: jeffrey.agrell@gmail.com

Preparatory Kopprasch Etudes

Introduction

The original Kopprasch etudes (ca. 1830) for horn are simple in both their rhythmic and harmonic content, but technically they are fairly challenging; they are not for beginners in any case. Young players must amass some years of experience on their instrument before they are ready to take on Kopprasch.

Preparatory Kopprasch provides novice players with the chance to work on the same basic techniques as the originals, but years earlier. PK etudes are constructed as to be accessible to anyone who has played horn for about a year or more. PK etudes achieve this by being shorter in length and limited in range, as well as having more frequent chances to breathe (rests!). Note values and meters have also been adjusted to be more user friendly. Teachers of horn may use some, many, or all of them as the foundation for a strong set of basic skills so that your student will be ready to tackle the original Kopprasch etudes much earlier and more successfully than was possible before.

More advanced (Kopprasch-savvy) players may also find this collection to be something of an appetizing assortment of sight-reading snacks for warm-up, warm-down, brush-up on the basics, or just plain fun (see if you can sight-read these *perfectly* the first time through. Did it? Well done! Now do it again, but transposed in E, Eb, D, C, G, etc.).

Notes on the Etudes

Unlike the originals, very few tempo markings or dynamics are given here. The purpose is to provide the teacher with the chance to have the student play the etudes at a variety of different tempos and dynamics, from slow and soft to faster and louder. Articulation is also another candidate for variation. Rhythms are similar to the originals throughout; teachers are also encouraged to have their students try out a variety of rhythms, not just the printed ones. Teachers and students in traditional studies have all the decisions like this made for them already; it is a feature here, not a bug, that you have something to say about these basic parameters. So: get out your pencil and customize each etude!

Note that this set of etudes is, like the originals, mostly progressive. Challenges, length, and range gradually increase over the collection. One area that PK occasionally adds that is less common than in the original is a greater variety of keys, the idea being that as long as the range is comfortable for the player, having notes in less familiar keys won't present a problem, and can make those tricky keys much more familiar and friendly by this early exposure.

Commentary on the Content of Each Etude

1 – Diatonic scale exercise. Range is G3 to A4. Keys visited during this slow etude include C, G, G7, E, A, A7, D, Dm.

2 – Scales in thirds. Range is A3 to A4. Keys visited: C, Bb, B, Db

3 – Diatonic scale movement, 3/4 meter. Key of C. We like to introduce transposition to novice students very early on. This etude could be transposed into E or Eb. Although many of the etudes in PK are suitable for transposition, this will be our only mention of transposition possibilities – each teacher and decide for themselves where they would like to assign transpositions.

4 – Diatonic scale exercise.

5 – Here the movement is between adjacent overtones using one "horn" (= one fingering, one length of tubing). "C horn", for instance, means use the fingering F:13 to select that length of tubing (that "horn"); the notes that are produced from overtones 8 to 9 are our (thinking in F) G4 to A4. The reason we practice exercises like this is because this is the way the horn really works is not the valves. The first order of business for every horn student is to learn to move the pitch up and down the overtone (or harmonic) series without valves (and preferably not using notation). This "mechanism" for moving the pitch is using a specific combination of change in air speed, lip muscle tension, and aperture size. Each line in this etude is done on one "horn", i.e. one length of tubing or fingering. Novice players need to learn the harmonic (or overtone) series from Day One so they can "think" in horn and "speak" horn. It is highly desirable that both teacher and student are "horn literate" in this way.

This exercise should be memorized as soon as possible.

6 – Scales in thirds. Keys: C, Db. It is written all staccato; it's a good idea to repeat it slurring the 8th note pairs.

7 – Major triads and scales. Keys visited: all of them.

8 – Major and minor triads. Range: G3 to C4.

9 – Key of F. First meeting with 16th notes in a repeating pattern (keep the tempo slow for a while in spite of the 16th notes). Groups of diatonic scale movement, mixed articulation. Some chromatic decoration of chord and nonchord tones.

10 – Diatonic scale patterns using the formula 3123 or 1321. Keys visited: C, Bb, B, D, G, Dm, C7, F.

11 – This etude is about enhancing control of finger movement of the valve levers.

12 – Keys: G, D, D7, Gm. Diatonic patterns: 8765 and 1234.

13 – 3/4 meter. Various major and minor triads that include a chromatic approach tone (CAT).

14 – 6/8 meter. More triad work with some CATs.

15 – 3/4 meter. Slow, lyrical waltz-like piece. Add slurs at will.

16 – Diatonic scale patterns plus minor or major third leaps. Harmonies: C major and C minor.

17 – 6/8 meter. Various triads (I, ii, IV, V7) in C major.

18 – Expanding intervals, built around various chords in C major (I, ii, iii, IV, V7)

19 – 3/4 meter. Key of Bb; modulation to Gm and back to Bb. Ascending diatonic scale patterns.

20 – Expanding intervals, both diatonic and chromatic.

21 – 3/4 meter. Major arpeggios and scales.

22 – Lyrical melody in 4/4 with a wide variety of note values.

23 – 3/4 meter. Triad arpeggios; featured interval: fifths, ascending and descending.

24 – "Bouncy" interval practice – expanding intervals.

25 – 6/8 meter. Bb major. Mostly triads in Bb major and its diatonic related keys.

26 – Major triads, using the rhythmic formula Short Short Long.

27 – G major, mostly, with the occasional CAT.

28 – Introduction of dotted rhythms, dotted 8th + 16th. Various key visited: Am, E7, C, G, Cm, Bb, Eb, Ab.

29 – Bb major. 4-note diatonic scale patterns that alternate ranges and direction. In the middle it changes to F minor and a brisker 3/4 meter. Top note is Db5.

30 – 6/8 meter. Eb major.

31 – Features the diatonic pattern 1235, plus a few arpeggios and CATs.

32 – Interval leaps using drone notes between chord or scale tones.

33 – Only two rhythms for the whole piece: quarter slurred to an eighth note using various intervals.

34 – Flowing piece that alternates minor and major chords and mixes interval leaps, arpeggios, and diatonic scales in several keys.

35 – Features octave scales. Keys of C, G7, B, Bb, A, Ab.

36 – Scales in 3rds, mostly. Second half sees daring excursions into diminished arpeggios and C natural minor.

37 – Major arpeggios explored using the pattern 1 3 (thirds).

38 – 12/8 meter. Key of C minor. One measure of chromatic scale movement. Middle section: wide intervals. Last section shifts to C major + CAT decoration of the G triad.

39 – Ab major. Arpeggiated chord tones.

40 – 6/8 meter. Leap followed by repeated (triad) note.

41 – CAT festival (chord tones decorated by chromatic approach tones). F major. Some rhythmic challenges in the rests, no extra charge.

42 – 3/4 meter. Basic arpeggiated chords in C major.

43 – 6/8 meter. Triads followed by repeated 5th scale degree, often decorated with neighboring tones (chromatic or diatonic). Also featured: diatonic and chromatic scale work.

44 – Natural horn (overtone) time. Similar to Etude #5. It provides practice moving the pitch between two adjacent overtones using various rhythms. Use the "mechanism" (air, lip tension, aperture) to make the pitch change, not the left arm (mouthpiece pressure).

Reminder: the "C horn" designation refers to the length of tubing that enables us to move from G4 to A4; this length is produced by one fingering, F:13. These notes are overtones 8 and 9, which are always our first choice when we play traditional lip trills. This etude is thus really a proto-trill exercise for young players. Note that all of the pairs of adjacent overtones here are adjacent 8 to 9 movements (the last two lines are 9 to 8). The different "horns" have nothing to do with transposition; they indicate the fingering (which gives a certain length of tubing, i.e. pitch of the fundamental) to use to access the adjacent pairs of overtones 8 and 9.

45 – First part is in C minor, with visits to several other keys. Some repeated patterns. Last part uses longer note values in C major.

46 – CATs usually appear on weak beats; they are featured on the strong beats here, decorating a note of a triad. Most C major with surprise guest appearances of diminished arpeggios.

47 – 6/8 meter. Lots of leaps of 3rds and 5ths. A couple CATs. C major and A minor.

48 – Features triplets and chromatic scales. Top note: D5. Merry prank ending.

49 – Slow and lyrical. Keys/chords visited: G, D7, Em, B7, Cm, G7, C.

50 – 12/8 meter. Lots of chord tones decorated with neighboring tones, either chromatic (CAT) or diatonic. Key areas: G, C, Am, F, D, G7.

51 – Features jumps from one chord tone to another, then decorates that second chord tone with a CAT. There are also stretches of interval jumps, mostly fifths. Last note: C2!

52 – C minor scales with some diatonic and chromatic decoration.

53 – 3/4 meter, G major, slow & lyrical.

54 – Straightforward basic arpeggio & scale work, up and down. Top note: E5. Key/chords visited: C, G, G7, E, Am, D7.

55 – Similar to 51 (CATS). Key areas visited: C, Cm, Db, G7, Ab Lydian, Eb. Chromatic scale G3 to G4. Last note is C2.

56 – 6/8 meter. Diatonic triad arpeggio sequences in C major. Last note: C4 or C3.

57 – Up and down (mostly) major arpeggios in a rainbow of keys: C, Am, F, Bb, Gm, Eb, Cm, Ab, Db, G. Optional C2 on the last note.

58 – Ascending (mostly) triad arpeggios. Keys visited: Bb, Bb dim., Dm, Gm, C7, F7, F, Bbm. Top note: F5.

59 – Slow and lyrical. G minor. Some 16th notes. Top note: G5(!).

60 – Up and back triad study, mostly in C and G. Variation: slur the 8th notes, in either two or four note groups. Top note: G5. Last note is C2.

Millennium Kopprasch Series

PREPARATORY KOPPRASCH
Horn Etudes

Jeffrey Agrell

Preparatory Kopprasch Etudes

1

(Keys: C, G, G7, E, A, A7, D, Dm)

2

(Keys: C, Bb, B, Db)

(Repeat in E, Eb transpositions)

4

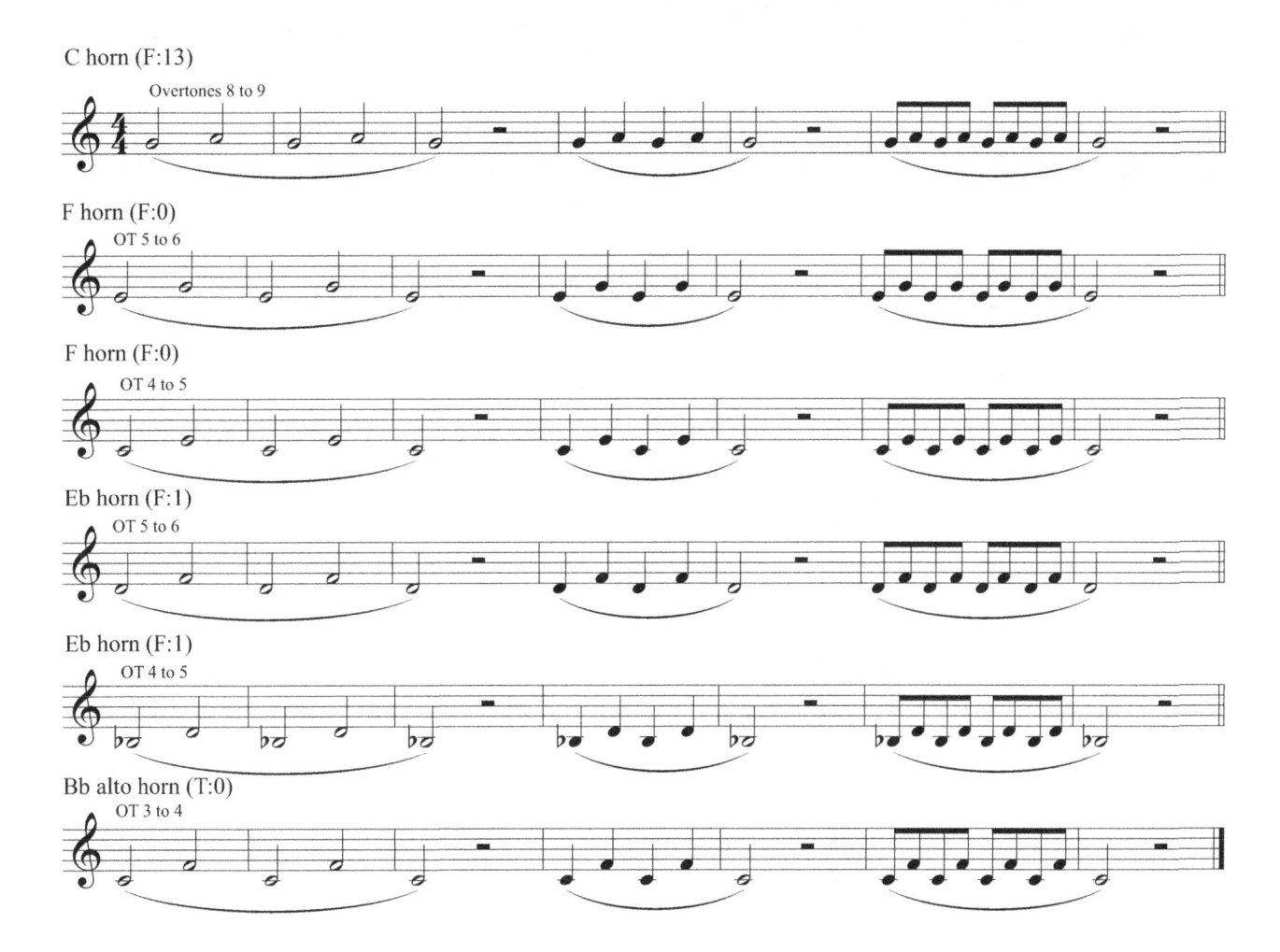

5

C horn (F:13) — Overtones 8 to 9

F horn (F:0) — OT 5 to 6

F horn (F:0) — OT 4 to 5

Eb horn (F:1) — OT 5 to 6

Eb horn (F:1) — OT 4 to 5

Bb alto horn (T:0) — OT 3 to 4

6

Repeat all, slurring 8th note pairs.

7

8

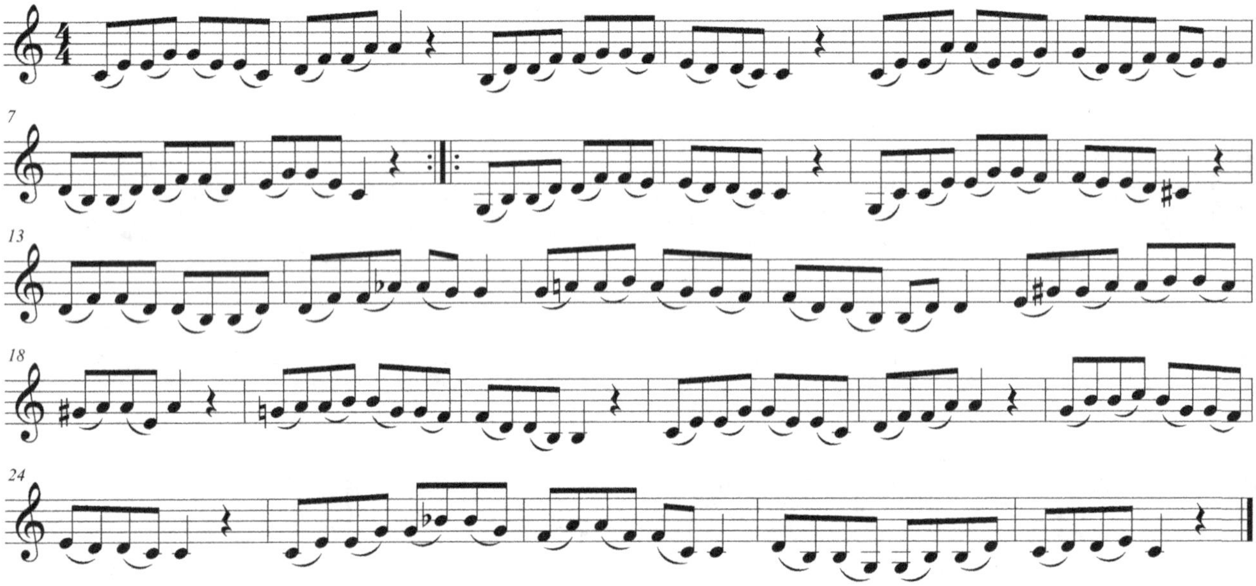

9

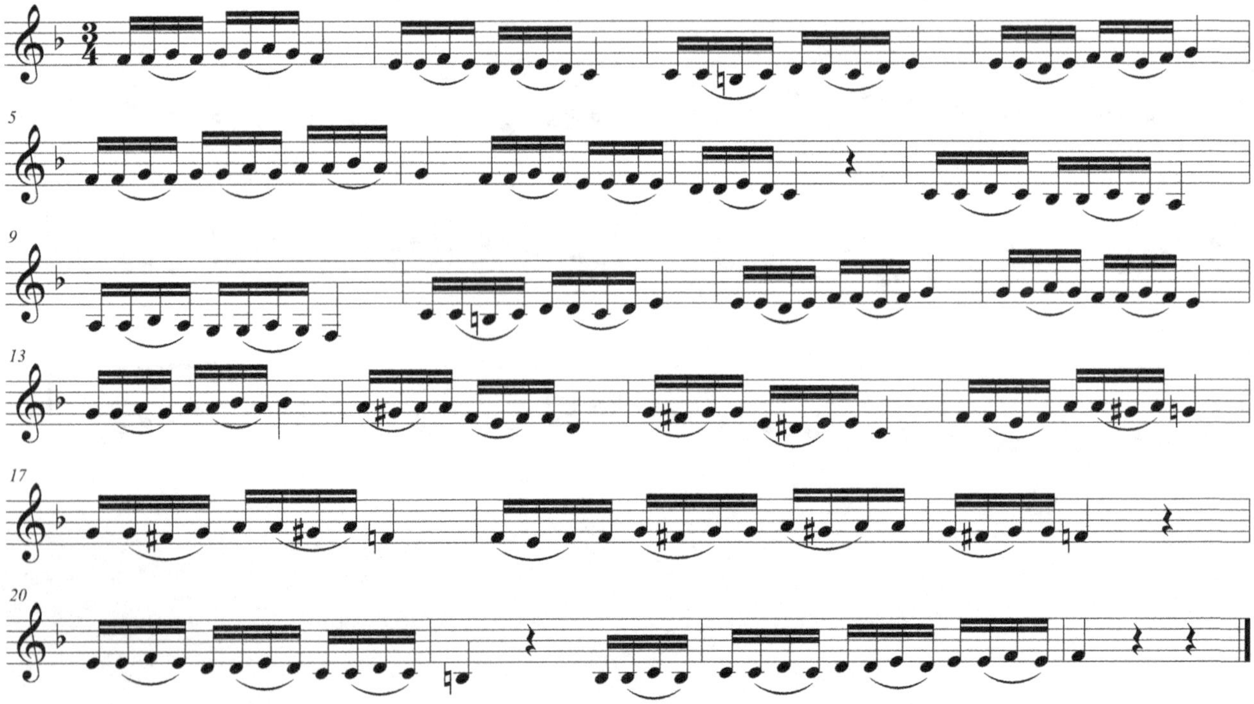

10

11

Practice slow to fast; repeat 16ths ad lib. Work on regularity and smoothness of transition between notes.
Practice both with trigger up and trigger down (fingerings are the same).

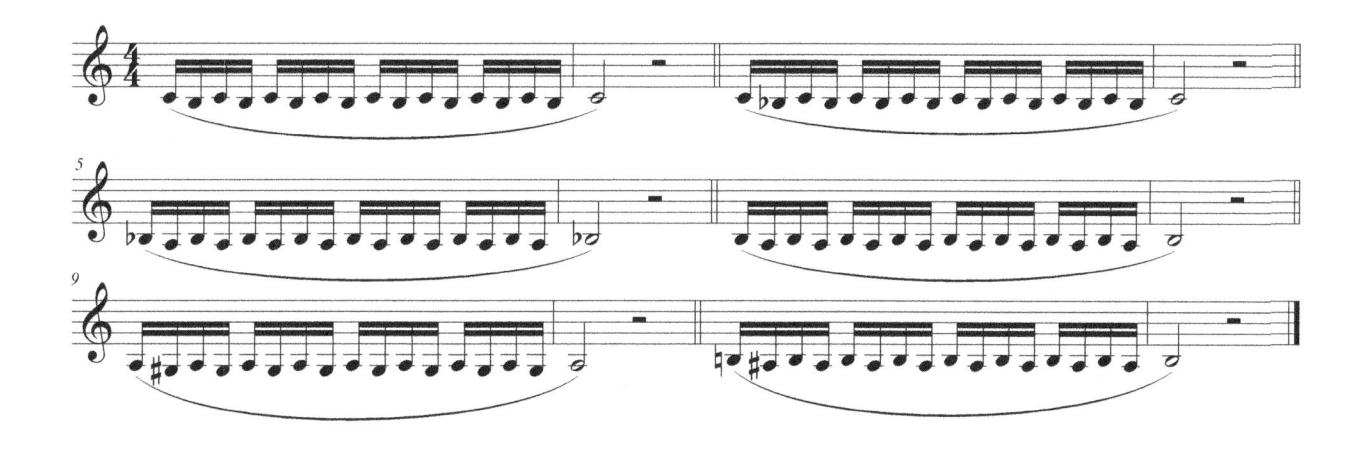

12

13

14

15

16

17

18

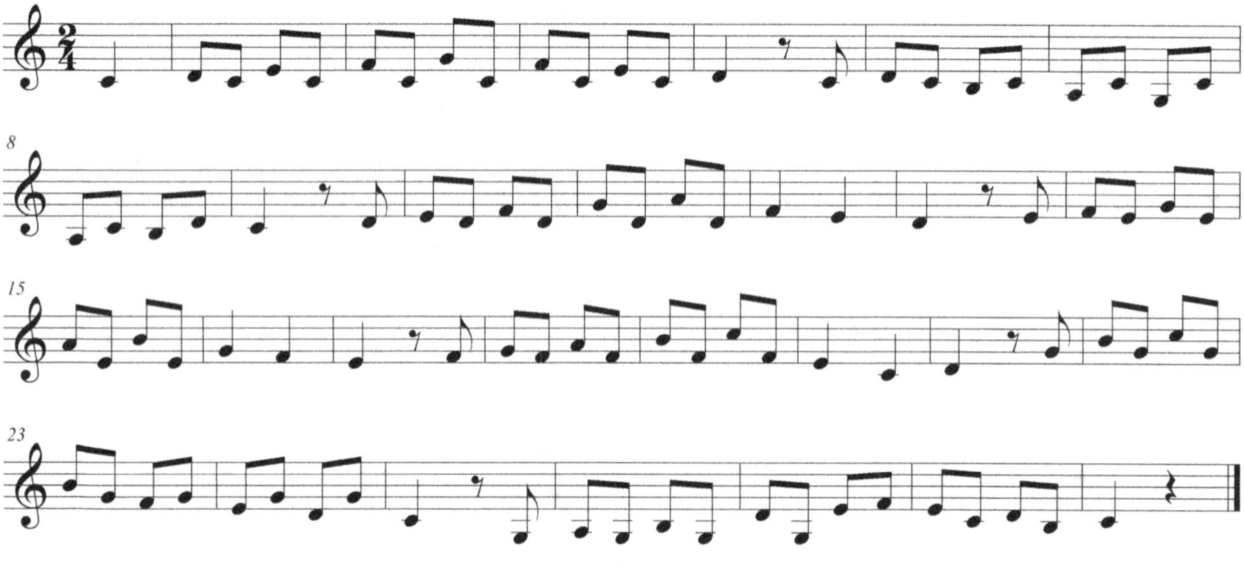

19

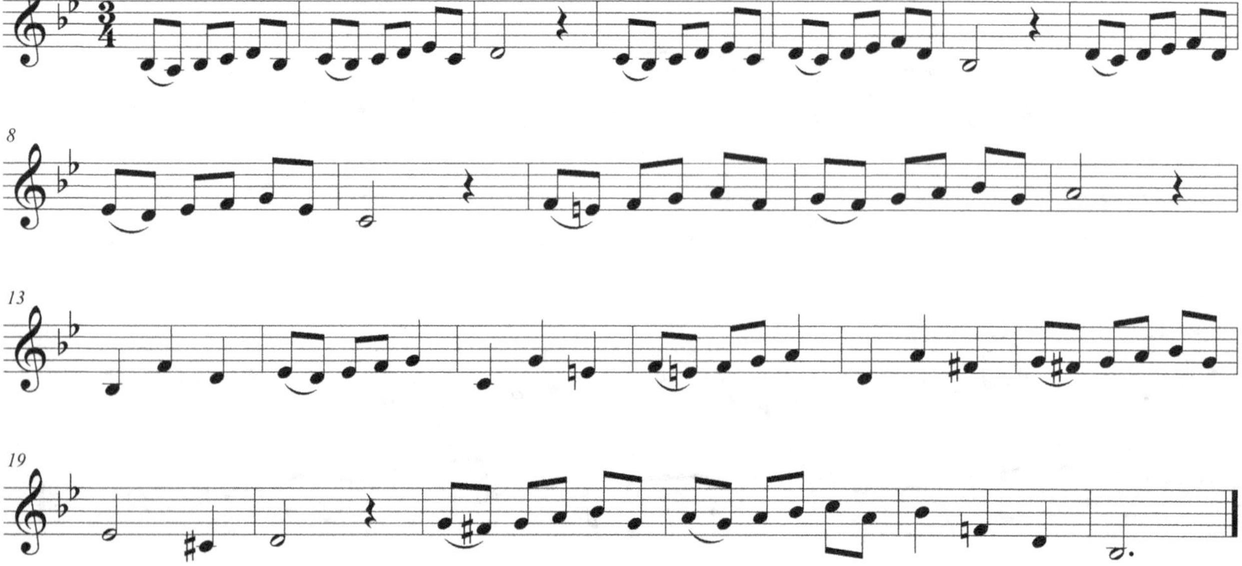

20

21

22

23

24

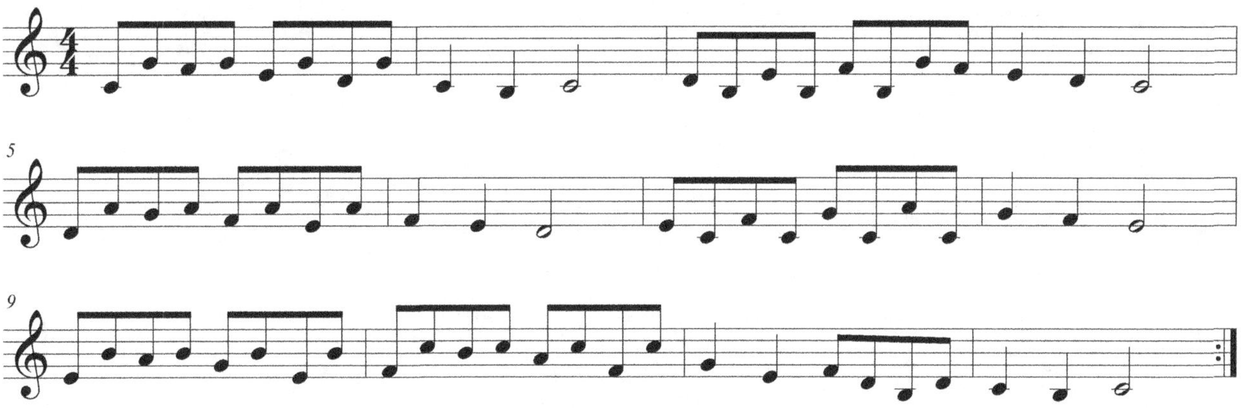

25

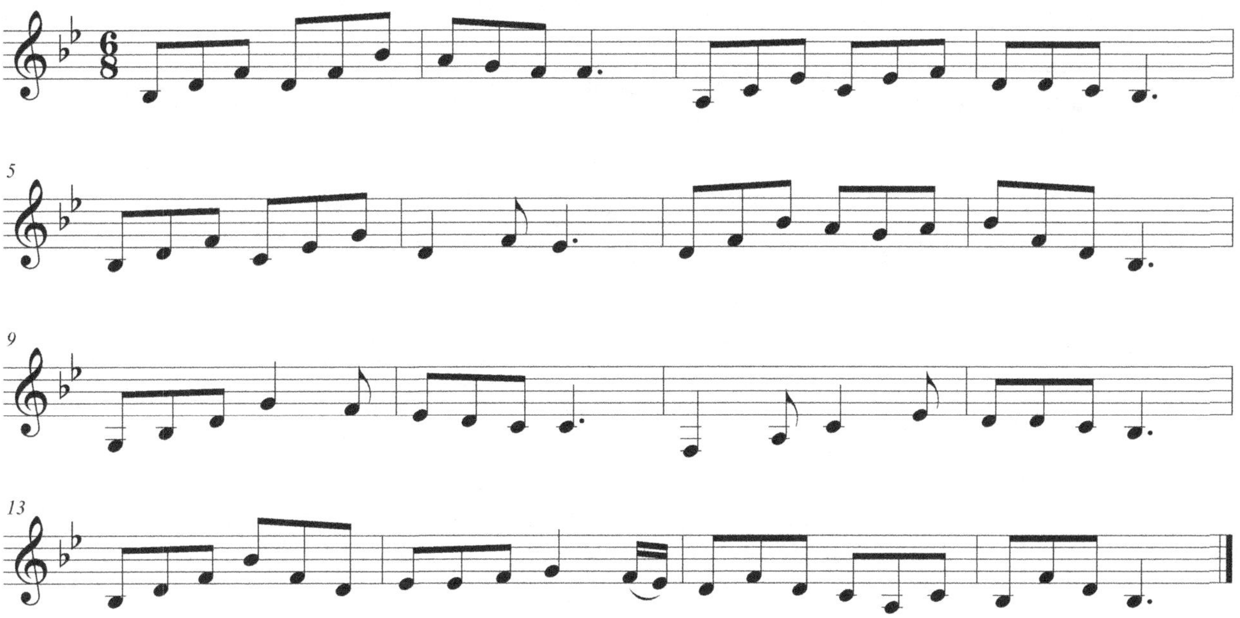

26

27

28

29

30

31

32

33

34

35

36

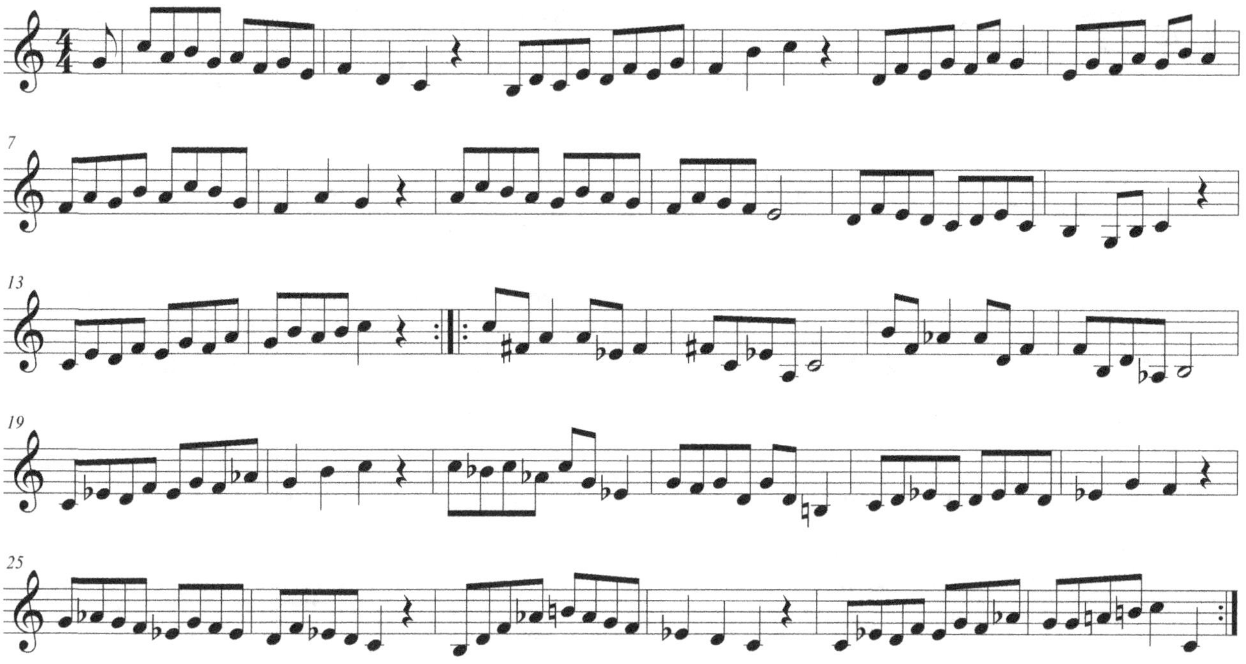

37

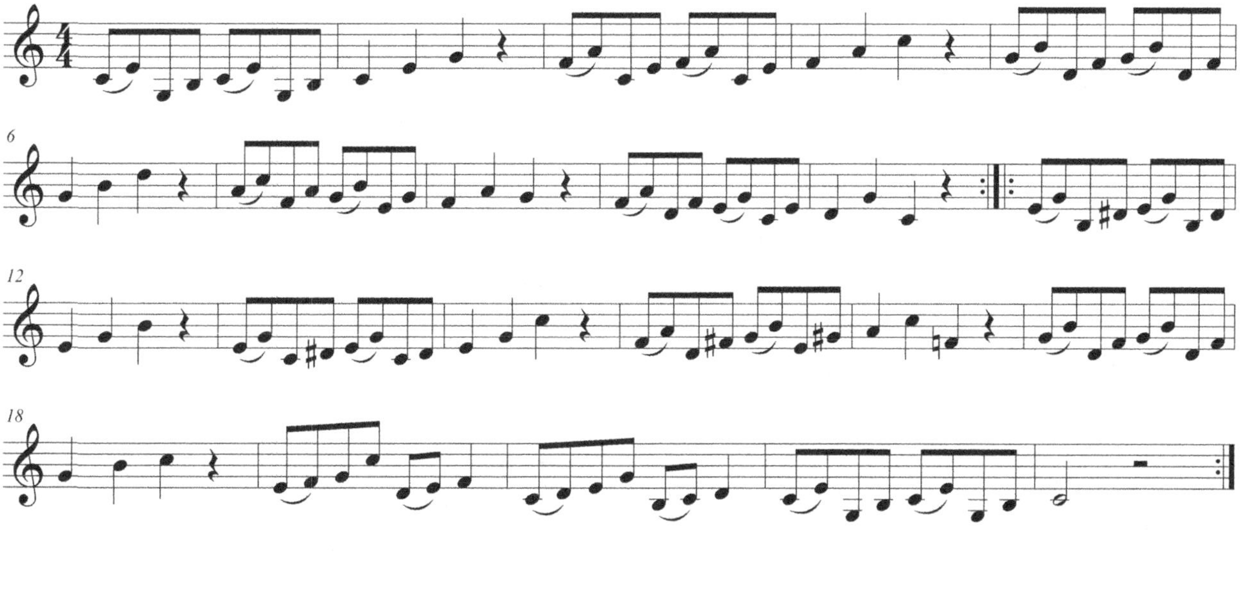

38

39

40

41

C.A.T.S.

42

43

44

All-Natural (Horn)

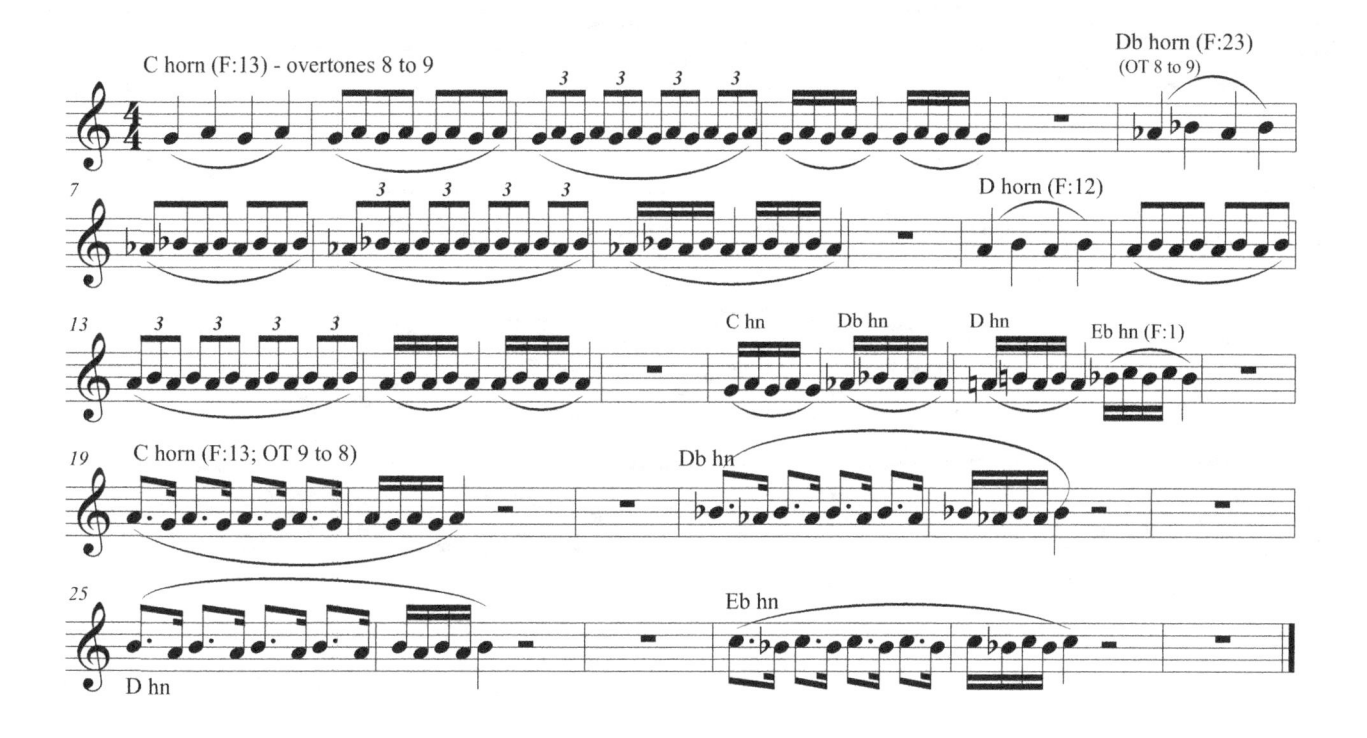

45

46

47

48

49

50

51

52

53

54

55

56

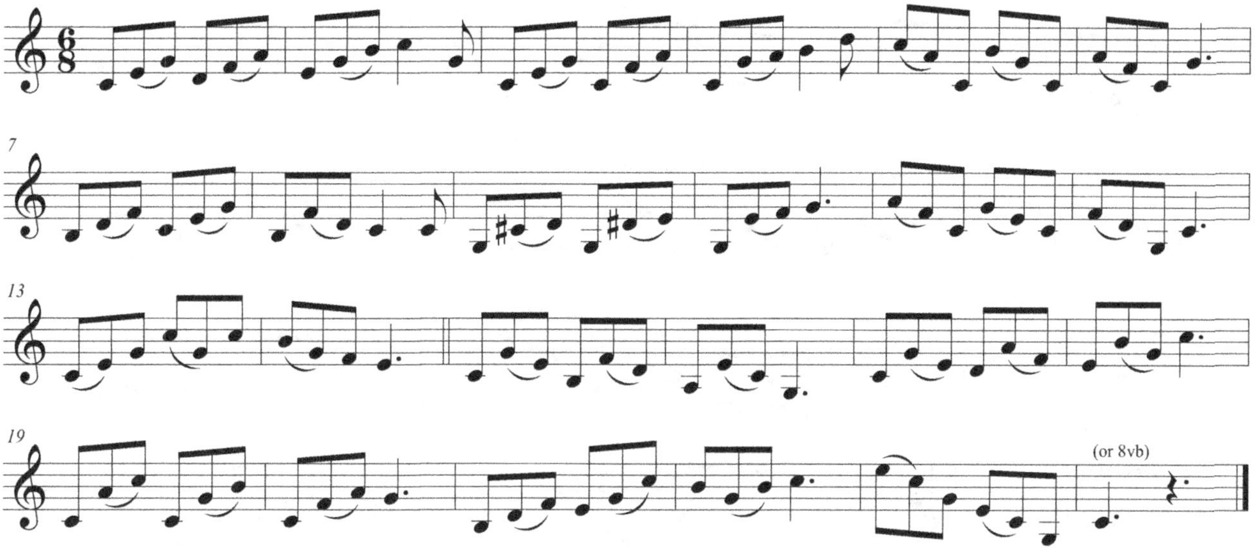

57

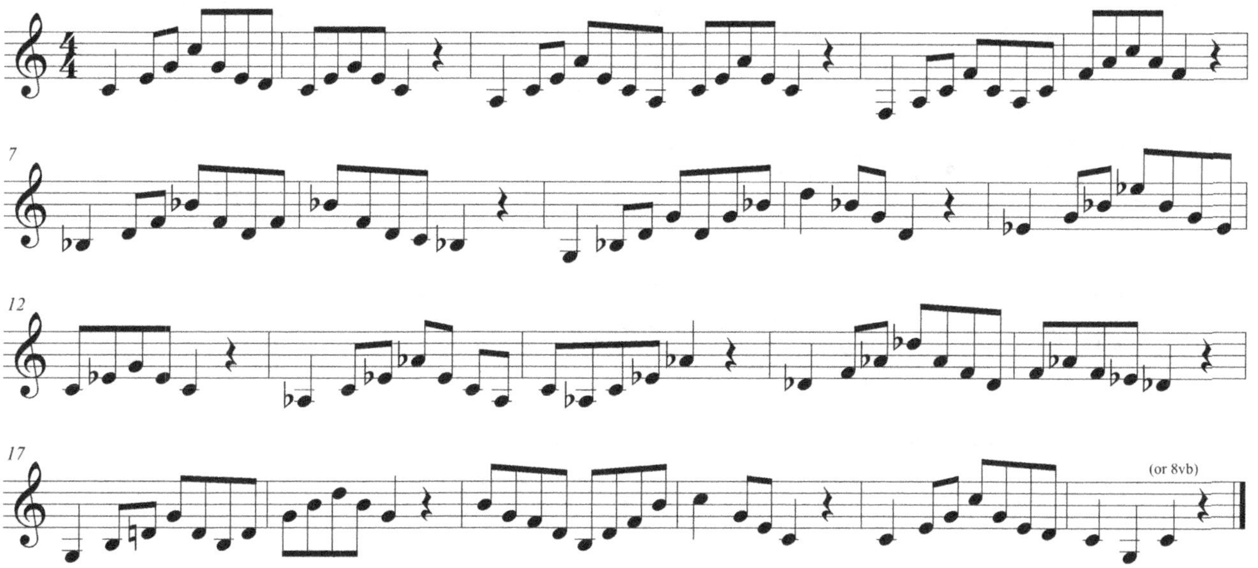

58

59

60

Variation: slur the 8th notes

About the Author

Jeffrey Agrell has earned his living playing and teaching horn since college. After a first career as a symphony orchestra musician, he has been horn professor at the University of Iowa since 2000.

He has performed and taught the full gamut of horn literature, including the repertoire for symphony orchestra, opera, musicals, ballet, operetta, and chamber music, while stretching personal artistic boundaries beyond the orchestra as a educator, composer, writer, clinician, recording artist, and solo performer. He is a former two-term member of the Advisory Council of the International Horn Society, has been a member of the faculty of the Asian Youth Orchestra in Hong Kong, and has taught at the prestigious Kendall Betts Horn Camp since 2005.

Besides performing, he has won awards as both a writer and composer, with well over one hundred published articles, dozens of published and recorded compositions, and many books to his credit, most recently, the Millennium Kopprasch Series *(Rhythm Kopprasch, Harmony Kopprasch)*, Horn Technique (447 p., 2017) and *The Creative Hornist* (228 p., 2017). He is an expert on classical improvisation, and has authored landmark books in this area, including *Improvisation Games for Classical Musicians*, Vol. I (2008) and Vol. II (2016).

Outside of horn and writing, he is a used-to-be amateur jazz guitarist, and currently an enthusiastic, if not particularly skilled conga drum player.

To contact Jeffrey Agrell with questions, comments, crazy ideas, get into interesting discussions about any of this, or engage him for concerts, workshops, keynote addresses, lectures, masterclasses, and all that, write to him at jeffrey.agrell@gmail.com

Made in the USA
Monee, IL
27 February 2024